W9-CRF-963

Science Explorers

FINDING OUT ABOUT

Whales

Elin Kelsey

Owl

Owl Books are published by Greey de Pencier Books Inc.,
179 John Street, Suite 500, Toronto, Ontario M5T 3G5

The Owl colophon is a trademark of Owl Children's Trust Inc.
Greey de Pencier Books Inc. is a licensed user of trademarks of Owl Children's Trust Inc.

Text © 1998 Elin Kelsey
Illustrations © 1998 Susan Nagy

All rights reserved. No part of this book may be reproduced or copied in any form without written consent from the publisher.

Distributed in the United States by Firefly Books (U.S.) Inc.,
230 Fifth Avenue, Suite 1607, New York, NY 10001

We acknowledge the generous support of the Canada Council for the Arts and the Ontario Arts Council for our publishing program.

Author's Dedication
For my favorite storytellers: Alanna, Fiona, Marielle, Sylvie, Matthias and Lucas.

Cataloguing in Publication Data

Kelsey, Elin
Finding out about whales

(Science explorers series)
ISBN 1-895688-79-5 (bound)   ISBN 1-895688-80-9 (pbk.)

1. Whales – Juvenile literature.   I. Title.   II. Series.

QL737.C4K44 1998   j599.5   C97-932602-8

Design & Art Direction: Julie Naimska (original concept and design, text and cover);
Virginia Morin (text layout); Jean Peters (final design, text and cover)
Illustrations by Susan Nagy

Photo Credits
Front cover, Joel Rogers/Tony Stone Images; 6–7, Mark Jones/Minden Pictures; 4, 5, 8, 9 (upper and lower), 11 (upper and lower), 24–25, 26, 27 (upper and lower), 28 (lower), 29 (lower), Flip Nicklin/Minden Pictures; 10, Richard Sears; 12–13, 18–19, 20 (inset photo), 23 (inset photo), 28 (upper), 30–31, 35, 36–37, 37, John K. B. Ford/Ursus Photography; 4 (upper), 14 (upper and lower), 15 (upper and lower), 16 (upper and lower), 38, Fred Sharpe; 17, 20 (right), Graeme Ellis/Ursus Photography; 21 (upper), 22, 23 (upper), K. Ottnad; 21 (lower), Wayne Perryman; 32 (upper and lower), 34, 36 (left), J. L. Barrett-Lennard; 33 (upper and inset photo), John K. B. Ford; back cover, Fred Sharpe, author photo, Andrew Johnson.

Printed in Hong Kong

A   B   C   D   E   F

Contents

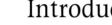

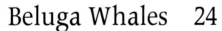

INTRODUCTION

Have you ever peered over the side of a boat and wondered about the animals that live beneath the sea? If you're very lucky, you might hear the "pppufff" of a whale's blow off in the distance. But look fast! Before you can count "three steamboats" the whale will have disappeared.

Imagine how tough it must be to study the lives of whales. They spend such little time at the surface and travel so far from shore that very few people ever see them. Whales are so difficult to study that when your parents were your age, nearly everything known about whales was learned by looking at their skeletons!

Luckily, some people weren't satisfied with that. When they heard the "puff" of a whale's blow, they wanted to know how long a whale could hold its breath. The sight of a group of whales travelling together made them wonder if individuals could be identified by the shape of their tails or the color of their fins. If you like to look at things in unexpected ways, to ask good questions and to develop creative ways to find answers to them, you've got the makings of an excellent whale researcher.

Thanks to their never-ending curiosity and patience, researchers are discovering things about whale life they never could have imagined. Sit next to a group of them swapping stories in a restaurant booth and you'll hear tales of seventy-year-old grandmothers, the growing pains of teenagers and the antics of mischievous two-year-olds. Like relatives at a family reunion, they compare memories of certain individuals and events. Don't be surprised if you have trouble figuring out when they're talking about people and when they're talking about *whales!*

So how did they go from assembling skeletons on a beach to discovering that teenaged male killer whales babysit their younger brothers and sisters? That's what this book is about.

In the following chapters you'll meet five species of whales that researchers are currently studying, and get a taste of the fascinating methods they're using to understand them even better.

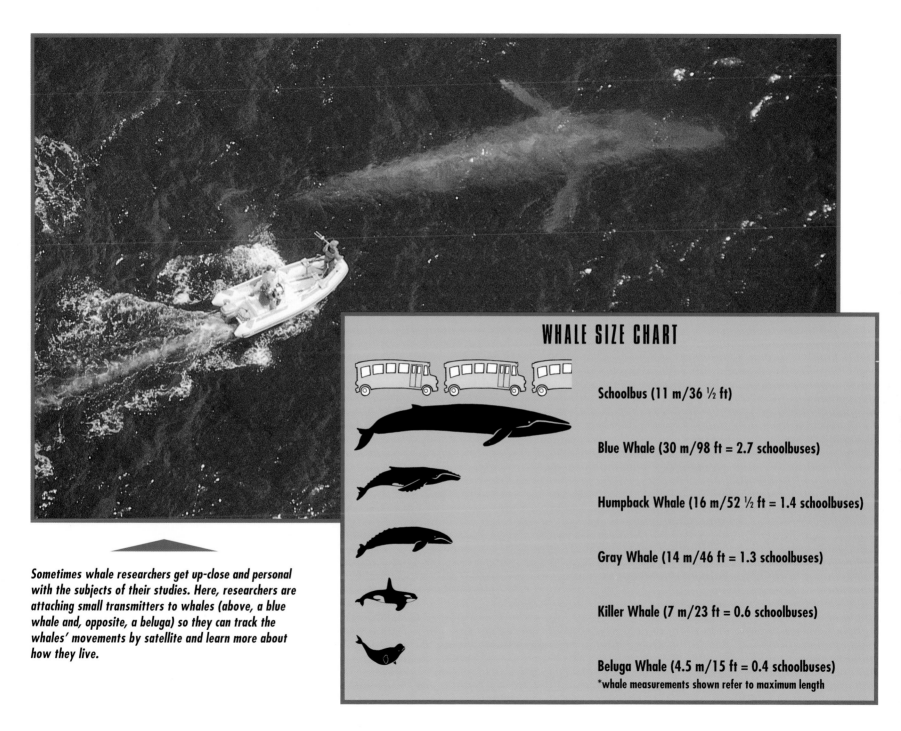

Sometimes whale researchers get up-close and personal with the subjects of their studies. Here, researchers are attaching small transmitters to whales (above, a blue whale and, opposite, a beluga) so they can track the whales' movements by satellite and learn more about how they live.

WHALE SIZE CHART

Schoolbus (11 m/36 ½ ft)

Blue Whale (30 m/98 ft = 2.7 schoolbuses)

Humpback Whale (16 m/52 ½ ft = 1.4 schoolbuses)

Gray Whale (14 m/46 ft = 1.3 schoolbuses)

Killer Whale (7 m/23 ft = 0.6 schoolbuses)

Beluga Whale (4.5 m/15 ft = 0.4 schoolbuses)
*whale measurements shown refer to maximum length

Blue Whales

• How do we find them?

How do we count them?

RESEARCH NOTES

Scientific name: *Balaenoptera musculus*

- Blue whales are the largest animals in the world. An average male is as long as a basketball court, and the females are even larger.

- Researchers identify individual blue whales by the skin color patterns on the side of the dorsal (back) fin.

- Blue whales are found in every ocean of the world, from the north pole to the south pole.

- Blue whales usually travel alone or in pairs.

- Each day during the feeding season, a blue whale can consume enough food to fill 64,000 cereal bowls. They eat shrimp-like animals so tiny, several could rest on a grain of rice.

- Blue whales are one of the group of "baleen" whales, named after the baleen plates on their upper jaws. Baleen is a material that is similar to your fingernails, and filters small fish and other animals from the water.

How do we find them?

It's Dinnertime!

Microscopic animals called zooplankton live in thick swarms near the ocean surface (see inset photo on right). When a blue whale spots a swarm, it expands its mouth and sucks in several tons of water. Then it closes its mouth and forces the water out through baleen plates, which look like the teeth on a giant comb. The baleen traps thousands of the minuscule animals—a nice mouthful for the whale.

Close your eyes and try to identify all of the sounds you can hear. It's difficult, isn't it? Imagine how much harder it would be to recognize sounds in an environment you had never seen before. That's the challenge facing a team of scientists who are trying to recognize blue whales in the north Pacific Ocean by the sound of their calls.

To listen for blue whales, the first thing a researcher needs is the right equipment. The U.S. Navy uses underwater microphones, called *hydrophones*, to follow submarines in the north Pacific. With these hydrophone systems they can pick up sounds more than 1,600 kilometres (1,000 miles) away. For the first time, the Navy is allowing a team of whale researchers to listen in on their hydrophone systems. The whale researchers are hoping to find out where blue whales spend their time by tracking the sound of their calls. The only trouble is, no one is quite sure which sounds are being made by blue whales!

These photographers will have to be careful with this shot because they may have to wait a half-hour to take another one. When a blue whale's tail rises up and out of the water, it's a sure sign that the whale is going down, down, down for a dive. One look at the size of this tail and you can begin to imagine the 80 tons of whale that came before it.

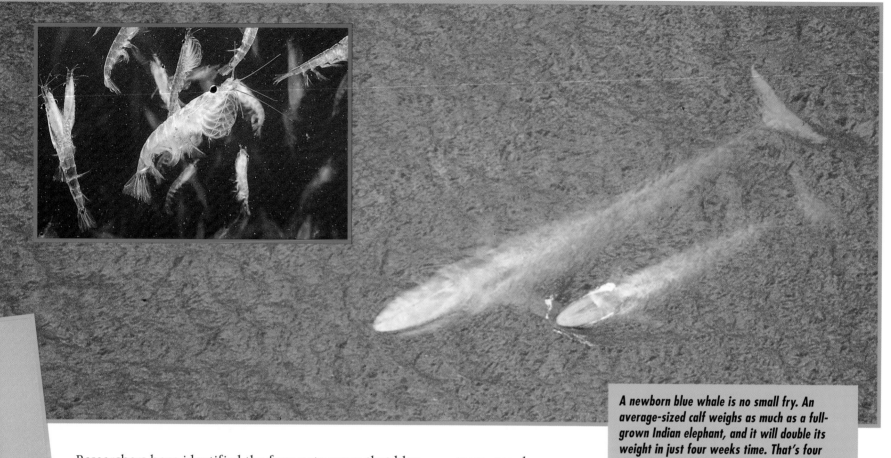

Researchers have identified the four-note songs that blue whales use as calls. But even if a blue whale was resting right by your boat singing one of them, chances are you wouldn't hear it. Many of the sounds that blue whales make are too deep and low in frequency to be heard by human ears. So how do researchers examining the Navy hydrophone recordings detect these low frequency sounds? They use computers to translate the sounds into wave pictures, called *sonograms*. By looking at these sonograms, or *voice prints,* scientists can see what they can't hear.

Once you can hear, or see, the sounds of a blue whale, identifying them should be easy, right? Unfortunately, the answer is "no." As the research team records more blue whale calls, it gets more complicated to identify the whales by the calls. The researchers have found that blue whales living in the south Pacific have a deeper call than blue whales living in the north Pacific. In fact, north Pacific blue whales sound a lot like a different kind of whale altogether, the fin whale. The researchers are hoping to spend more time at sea recording the calls of whales in the next phase of their research project, to make better sense of the intriguing sounds captured by the Navy's submarine trackers.

A newborn blue whale is no small fry. An average-sized calf weighs as much as a full-grown Indian elephant, and it will double its weight in just four weeks time. That's four times faster than a human baby grows. It takes a lot of calories to grow so quickly. Blue whale calves nurse from their mothers for several months. The milk that they drink is 35–50% fat—it's so rich and thick, it makes a double-scoop ice cream milkshake look slimming!

How do we count them?

Blue whales are so big, you might not think researchers would have a problem counting them. But counting blue whales in the enormous area of the world's oceans is like counting tiny minnows in a lake. One method of counting blue whales, known as a line-transect study, follows the same principle you might use when searching for a missing contact lens on a basketball court. Rather than randomly rushing from one spot to another, you'll have the best luck if you slowly walk in straight lines up and down the court until you've covered all the floor space.

Each summer, blue whales gather to feed in the deep canyons off the central coast of California. Researchers believe it's the greatest concentration of blue whales in the world. By steering their boats in straight lines and travelling back and forth through the hundreds of square kilometres used by the whales, the researchers try to systematically count the number of whales in the area. You have to have a steady stomach for this kind of work. Peering through high-powered binoculars while perched near the top of a ship that is pitching up and down in heavy seas is a recipe for sea sickness. And your eyesight has to be excellent. The average distance between blue whale and whale spotter is 8 kilometres (5 miles).

Learning from Bones

It's sad that researchers know far more about dead blue whales than they do about living ones. Most of the information about where blue whales live and how their bodies work was collected from the more than 300,000 blue whales killed before hunting was banned— just thirty years ago.

10

Recent line-transect surveys suggest that approximately 1,800 north Pacific blue whales summer off the coast of California. How accurate is this count? No one knows for sure. It's easy to miss whales and impossible to know if you are counting the same whale more than once. It will be many years before all of the blue whales that summer in this area are catalogued, and more still before scientists will know if the population estimates are correct.

Each year, blue whales travel to the polar ice zones where they eat and eat and eat. Each day during the four-month feeding season, these 80 ton giants consume 200,000 times more calories than you do!

Imagine what it would be like if you could hear people speaking in other countries without the aid of a telephone. Low frequency calls of blue whales travel so much farther and faster through water than they would through the air that researchers using hydrophones (underwater microphones) have been able to eavesdrop on blue whale calls from thousands of kilometres away.

Humpback Whales

•Why do they blow bubbles?

How do they hunt?

Scientific name: *Megaptera novaeangliae*

- With long fore-flippers outstretched like wings, humpbacks lift their bodies above the water's surface into the air.

- Humpbacks have large pleated throats and baleen plates to filter small fish and other animals from the water.

- A humpback whale's tail is so wide, you couldn't fit it in your bedroom.

- The shapes and color patterns of a humpback whale's tail are as distinctive as people's fingerprints.

- More than 3,500 individual humpback whales can be identified by photographs of the undersides of their tail flukes.

- Humpback whales travel thousands of kilometres each year from sub-tropical mating areas to summer feeding grounds in the northern, southern and polar seas.

- Humpback whales spend most of their time alone or in mother-calf pairs, meeting in groups of about fifteen individuals in their feeding and breeding areas.

Why do they blow bubbles?

Humpback whales blow bubbles ranging in size from small enough to get under the shell of a shrimp to as big as a party-sized pizza. But not all the bubbles come out of their mouths. Like all whales, humpbacks breathe through an opening called a blowhole on the back of their heads. Tightening the muscles around its blowhole changes the shape of the opening, and the size of the bubbles that come out.

Fred Sharpe had seen groups of humpbacks blowing bubbles off the south-eastern coast of Alaska, and suspected that bubble blowing helps the whales catch fish. But because humpback whales blow their bubbles five storeys beneath the surface (with as many as fifteen giant whales criss-crossing underwater at the same time) he couldn't see what was happening.

So instead of spending his time in a boat watching whales, Fred spent two years in a laboratory investigating bubbles. In the lab, with air hoses, water tubs, microphones, fish and a huge artificial flipper, Fred tested ideas and watched situations he could never see from a boat.

Humpback whales are the biggest underwater bubble-blowers in the world! Rising up and out of the water like space-bound schoolbuses, humpback whales are so immense it's difficult for researchers to get close enough to study how these whales use bubbles to catch fish. Researcher Fred Sharpe uses a bubble tank (see above) to test how fish react to the types of bubbles humpbacks blow.

With a flap of their large flippers and a snap of their tail, humpback whales can lift themselves up, up, up out of the water. It's an ideal way to get a whale-sized back scratch.

Fred found it wasn't just the bubbles that scared the fish. It was also the sound the whales made. If you wet your finger and run it around the top of a glass you make a sound much like the fishing call of a humpback whale. This hunting sound is within the range of sounds fish hear best. As soon as the fish hear the sound made by hunting humpbacks, Fred believes they stop feeding and crowd together into a tight bunch. Fred also discovered that humpbacks use their huge flippers to frighten fish. A feeding humpback will extend its flippers alongside its jaws, forming a giant scoop that causes the fish to swim into the whale's open mouth.

To see if his experimental findings matched what humpback whales do at sea, Fred took a break from the lab to watch whales. He used a sonar device to shoot "pings" of sound into the water and create sound pictures. These sonar scans showed him what was happening underwater. The challenge would be to get close enough to a frenzy of huge feeding whales to record the action! Fred had two goals for this phase of his study: to stay alive, and to not interfere with the feeding behavior he was trying to study.

Can you see any barnacles hitching a ride in this picture? Three different kinds of these small, shelled animals live on the throat, chin, fins and tails of slow-moving whales. Whale researchers can recognize some humpbacks by their "barnacle neckties."

15

How do they hunt?

Fred Sharpe's sonar studies proved some amazing things. It turns out that when a group of humpbacks gets together to feed, one whale takes the lead. That whale dives down beneath a school of fish, releases a stream of bubbles from its blowhole and emits a distinctive feeding sound. The fish move up to escape the sound, and the bubbles rise with them, forming a tube-shaped net that keeps the fish from swimming away. As the fish near the surface, the whales thunder up from below, filling their enormous mouths with the tons of fish corralled in the bubble nets.

When he began his research, Fred expected to find that all humpbacks make and use bubble nets the same way. Instead he discovered that bubble-netting is more like a team sport, in which the formation of the team and the plays called by the team captain change depending on what's happening in the game. Bubble nets vary in size and shape depending on which humpback whale is blowing the bubbles, how many whales are involved in the hunt and what kinds of fish they are hunting.

Bubble-Blowers

Humpbacks aren't the only animals who use bubbles. Seabirds, such as puffins and murres, blow bubbles through their nostrils to chase fish away from the safety of their schools. River otters blow bubbles when they're trying to flush crabs from tight hiding places. And some scientists believe that beluga whales use trails of bubbles as underwater exclamation marks!

16

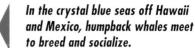

In the crystal blue seas off Hawaii and Mexico, humpback whales meet to breed and socialize.

Do humpbacks have partners or teams that they like to hunt with? Off south-east Alaska where Fred does his research, some humpbacks stay in the area all summer long and others simply pass through. According to Fred, certain whales often hunt together, but it appears to be a case of "the more, the merrier." The whales seem to look for new recruits and will adjust the size of the net they create to accommodate the number of whales joining in the hunt. Herring, which make up an important part of a humpback's diet, are strong, fast fish. Fred thinks the whales have learned it's easier to catch them using a bigger net and more whales to block fish escape routes.

In hundreds of hours of observation, Fred has never seen whales squabble for better positions around a net. Bubble-net hunting is a beautiful example of cooperative team work. How do the humpbacks communicate with each other during the hunt? Fred's studies show that they don't use vocalizations to communicate while hunting. He believes they watch each other, keep in close physical contact and listen to the sound of other whales moving through the water to make sure that they are all in sync.

When a humpback whale is lunge feeding, it expands its throat to take in huge amounts of seawater. By closing its mouth and lifting its enormous tongue, the whale forces the water out through its baleen plates, leaving fish and other marine food trapped behind. During the feeding season, humpback whales feast and feast and feast. An average-sized adult may consume more than a ton of fish each day!

Gray Whales

How do they find their way?

How do we track them?

Scientific name: *Eschrichtius robustus*

- A gray whale can grow as heavy as a military tank and twice as long as a telephone pole.

- Gray whales suck up mouthfuls of tiny animals and mud from the sea bottom, making marks that look like a giant ice cream scoop has dug the ocean floor.

- These large baleen whales have been known to wrap their mouths over huge stems of seaweed, removing the plants and animals that live on it with a mighty sluuuuurrrrppppp!

- The orange and gray markings are lice and barnacles that live on the gray whales' skin. They look creepy but they don't appear to harm the whales.

- When gray whales approach a small boat in search of a pat, they can be as gentle as puppies. A researcher who studies gray whale communication believes the sound of an idling outboard motor may remind the whales of the calls of other gray whales.

• How do they find their way?

Gray whale skin is a habitat for other animals. Flaky bits of "whale dandruff" are dinner for the whale lice (see inset photo below) that live on the whale.

Watching migrating gray whales is a lot like watching a parade, except that all of the floats are underwater. First come the adult females, then the adult males and, finally, mothers with their calves. They travel alone, in pairs or in small groups of twelve or so. Some rush ahead while others take up a steady pace as they journey from Mexico to Alaska and back again. During this annual migration a gray whale will swim the equivalent of 640,000 lengths of your community swimming pool.

How far do migrating gray whales travel each day? Researchers monitor gray whales with radio transmitters to find out. They've discovered that the distance travelled in a 24-hour time period varies from a few kilometres to well over 100 kilometres (60 miles).

Although stormy weather or areas where there is lots of boat traffic may cause individuals to take a slightly different course, gray whales appear to follow the same general migration route regardless of what time they are travelling. Mothers with calves, for example, follow a route that veers closer to the coast after it passes Los Angeles, California. The males and females travelling without calves follow a separate corridor that is farther from shore.

20

Researchers have watched gray whales poke their heads (and sometimes their whole bodies) out of the water when they are travelling around islands and complicated channels. They believe the whales are looking for familiar landmarks to tell them which route to follow. Navigating coastal waters is confusing business and sometimes whales do get lost—showing up in busy harbors or other areas where they are not normally found.

For the past twenty years, Jim Darling has been studying gray whales off the coast of Vancouver Island, British Columbia. From the thousands of identification photos he has taken, Jim and his colleagues have identified about one hundred individuals. Interestingly, now that they can recognize individuals, they've discovered that not all gray whales participate in the entire migration. Some return each year to favorite feeding areas along the BC coast rather than continuing the migration northward.

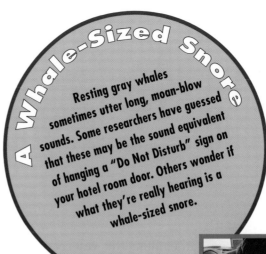

A Whale-Sized Snore

Resting gray whales sometimes utter long, moan-blow sounds. Some researchers have guessed that these may be the sound equivalent of hanging a "Do Not Disturb" sign on your hotel room door. Others wonder if what they're really hearing is a whale-sized snore.

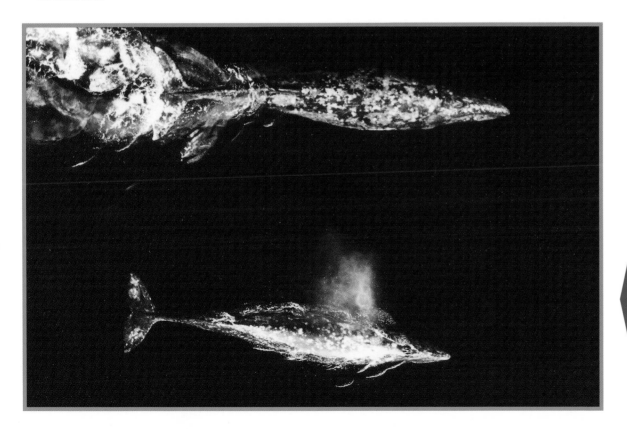

Researchers sort through pebbles and sand from the ocean floor in search of shells, scales and body parts, which help them to identify the tiny snails, worms and other undersea animals that gray whales eat.

Can you tell which whale is pregnant? If you guessed the upper one, you're right. Pregnant gray whales look wider when you see them from above. By comparing "fat" whales with "skinny" whales, researchers Wayne Perryman and Meghan Donahue are able to make rough guesses about the number of pregnant whales in the migrating population.

How do we track them?

Each spring, millions of people gather along the west coast of Canada and the United States to watch gray whales migrate. But often the only hint that a whale is near is the "blow" that rises from the surface of the water when it exhales.

Why is it possible to see a whale's blow? For the same reason you can see your own breath on a chilly day. When the warm air that you exhale comes into contact with the colder air around you, moisture trapped in your breath is released. The tiny droplets of water form the fine mist you can see.

Counting the blows of migrating gray whales on a typical wet day on the west coast is challenging work. Counting them at night used to be virtually impossible. Now, researchers Meghan Donahue and Wayne Perryman have discovered a way to find out how many gray whales pass the research stations when it is too dark to see them.

Whale watchers look for the distinctive heart shape of a gray whale's blow to count the number of whales in the area—just as bird watchers use sounds or flight patterns to identify and count birds when they are difficult to see individually.

Do Gray Whales sleep?

Not in the way we think of it. Like all whales, gray whales are voluntary breathers. They have to wake up each time they need to take a breath, and so they can only "sleep" for the few minutes that pass between breaths. Although gray whale researchers see mothers with calves quietly resting at the surface for short periods, it seems that migrating adults just keep going, and going....

22

Gray whale baleen is as thick and dense as a straw broom. It is strong and flexible enough to filter the mud, rocks and tiny animals the whales slurp up from the ocean floor.

Using a special camera called a thermal imager, Wayne and Meghan track whales at night by the heat of their blows. The thermal imager is so sensitive to temperature, it can detect the difference in heat generated by a bird and by a whale as far as 8 kilometres (5 miles) away. Rather than realistic pictures of gray whales, the thermal imager records "heat spots" that show up as fuzzy splotches on the video.

So do the whales travel all night, or do they spend the wee hours sleeping or visiting with one another? The videos reveal that gray whales migrate farther during the night than they do during the day. Yet anytime, day or night, they swim about as fast as you walk. What's happening? By watching the behavior of gray whales during the day and comparing it to the night video recordings, Meghan and Wayne believe that gray whales spend more time playing and mating during the day when they can see each other.

Beluga Whales

- What do they sound like?

- How well do they hear?

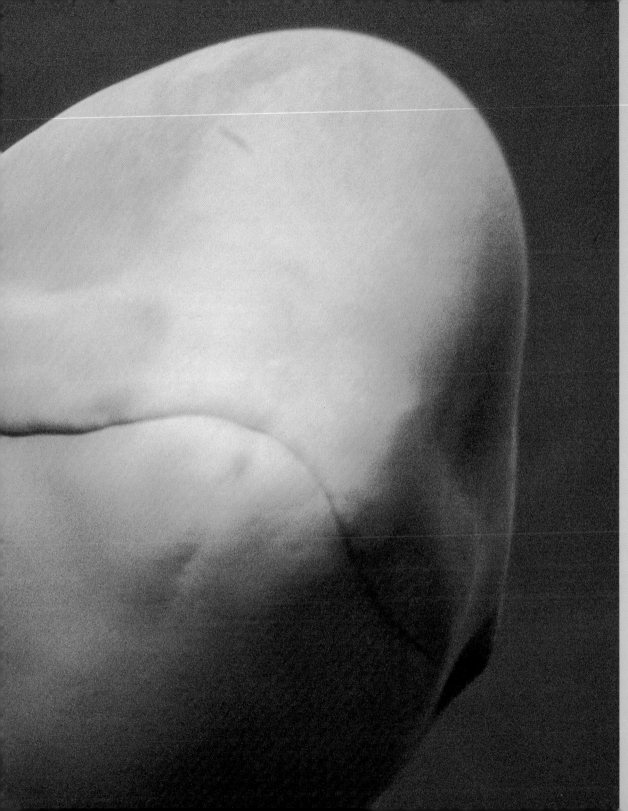

Scientific name: *Delphinapterus leucas*

- Belugas always seem to be smiling because of their fat, fleshy lips.

- Belugas are "toothed" whales, which means they have teeth, rather than baleen plates.

- An adult beluga is small enough to fit on a humpback whale's tail.

- A body weight that may be up to 30% fat helps a beluga living in near-freezing arctic waters maintain a warmer body temperature than yours.

- Belugas are dark gray when they're born and gradually become whiter. By the time they are adult, at the age of nine, most belugas are creamy white.

- Canada is home to many beluga populations made up of thousands of whales. But so many St. Lawrence River and Ungava Bay belugas have died from water pollution, these populations are classified as endangered.

•What do they sound like?

Research often leads scientists to discover things they never set out to find. That's what happened to Greg Dye and his colleagues at the John G. Shedd Aquarium in Chicago. They were working with dolphins in a hearing study, when their test subjects started to respond even when no test tones were being played. At first, the research team thought the equipment was malfunctioning or that the dolphins were confused. It took them a while to figure out the dolphins were hearing test tones—actually perfect imitations of them made by belugas in the neighboring pool.

What began as a test of dolphin hearing changed into a study of beluga mimicry. Using hydrophones (underwater microphones) in the whale exhibit, Greg recorded the belugas' squawks, squeals and whistles for forty hours. Then he transformed the sounds into pictures, called sonograms, to make it easier to compare the original sounds to new sounds the belugas might pick up.

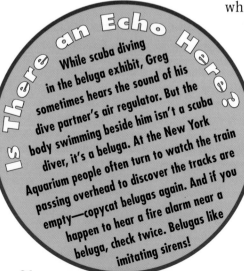

Is There an Echo Here?

While scuba diving in the beluga exhibit, Greg sometimes hears the sound of his dive partner's air regulator. But the body swimming beside him isn't a scuba diver, it's a beluga. At the New York Aquarium people often turn to watch the train passing overhead to discover the tracks are empty—copycat belugas again. And if you happen to hear a fire alarm near a beluga, check twice. Belugas like imitating sirens!

In the brilliant blue waters of a summer arctic sea, creamy white belugas appear to be dancers in an underwater ballet. Shy but curious, these belugas seem to be as interested in watching the underwater photographer, Flip Nicklin, as he is in watching them.

Understanding why belugas mimic sounds is tricky. Most belugas in the wild spend a good part of the year searching for areas of open water in a sea of shifting ice. Finding belugas is so difficult and expensive that almost nothing is known about what they do during the cold, dark arctic winter. It's easier to find them in summer when they gather in huge groups at the mouths of arctic rivers. But trying to identify individual beluga calls in a whole crowd of mimics is mind-boggling!

Even in aquariums, where researchers like Greg can get up close, it isn't easy to tell which beluga is making a sound. Unlike you, whales don't have vocal chords. Their calls don't come out of their mouths, so lipreading doesn't work. Belugas make some sounds by forcing air through their blowholes, so you might be able to see who's calling by following streams of bubbles. But many of the higher-pitched clicks and whistles leave no trace at all. These sounds travel invisibly straight out of the whales' foreheads.

Each summer, thousands of arctic belugas congregate in the warmer waters at the mouths of rivers to feed and socialize. Like teenagers at a rock concert, belugas often bob their heads up and out of the water to get a better look at the crowd (see above). Researchers call this behavior a "spy hop" because the whales "hop" up to "spy" a better view.

How well do they hear?

As Greg Dye listened to the beluga sounds he recorded in the aquarium, he was puzzled to hear the unmistakable calls of loons, wrens and thrushes on the tape. How had belugas in a Chicago aquarium learned to imitate birds living on the Pacific coast? The mystery was solved on a busy summer day when Greg walked beneath one of the aquarium's public address speakers. Can you guess what was playing on the speaker? West coast birds calls!

To trace how belugas learn new sounds, Greg first created three simple "whistles" that he knew the belugas did not know. Then he repeatedly played them for two seconds at a time. Using the hydrophones, he recorded the tones, and the belugas' attempts to imitate them.

Name-Calling

For many years researchers have wondered if every beluga has its own distinctive call. These "signature calls" would help belugas recognize one another when they gather in huge crowds. Some researchers suspect that by imitating another's call, a beluga is actually calling out the other's "name."

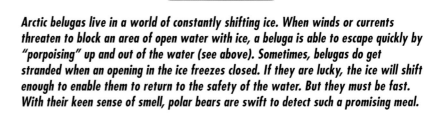

Arctic belugas live in a world of constantly shifting ice. When winds or currents threaten to block an area of open water with ice, a beluga is able to escape quickly by "porpoising" up and out of the water (see above). Sometimes, belugas do get stranded when an opening in the ice freezes closed. If they are lucky, the ice will shift enough to enable them to return to the safety of the water. But they must be fast. With their keen sense of smell, polar bears are swift to detect such a promising meal.

How do belugas respond to new sounds? First they listen. Then, they begin to "whistle along" with the tone as it's being played. They make lots of mistakes when they practice, often starting at the wrong pitch, or missing the tempo. In some cases, for example, if the tone drops from a high note to a low note, they pick up where the tone left off and imitate the sound dropping lower still. Eventually, they are able to do perfect accompaniments with the test tone. And then, finally, they can imitate the tone without any accompaniment at all.

Can you draw a beluga's ears without looking at a picture? Probably not. Most people have trouble remembering what whale ears look like because they're so difficult to see. A whale's ears are just two tiny holes on either side of its head. They're so small you couldn't fit a Q-Tip into them!

But, don't let the pint-sized pinholes fool you. Belugas appear to have remarkable hearing. While recording whale calls in the high arctic, John Ford watched a group of belugas suddenly stampede through the floating ice. What caused the whales to spook? From above water, everything appeared peaceful. John dipped his hydrophone into the water and listened. There it was, the faint whir of a mechanical engine. John searched the horizon for signs of a ship. Little did he realize he'd have to wait two and a half hours for the boat to arrive. The belugas had reacted to the sound of an icebreaker 84 kilometres (52 miles) away.

How many slate gray beluga calves can you count in this picture? Researchers use photos like these to count the number of new-borns in a population of belugas.

Killer Whales

- How do we tell them apart?
- How do different groups live?

Are they in danger?

RESEARCH NOTES

Scientific name: *Orcinus orca*

- Killer whales, also called "orcas," have distinctive black and white markings, and pointed fins on their backs.

- Killer whales can grow as long as two large canoes placed end to end.

- Killer whales are "toothed" whales. Some eat fish, others eat warm-blooded animals.

- Killer whales are the largest members of the group of animals we call "dolphins."

- Killer whales are found in all the world's oceans.

- Some killer whales live in pods led by the oldest female, known as the matriarch.

- Some male killer whales live with their mothers for their entire lives.

- Teenaged killer whales babysit their younger brothers and sisters.

- Sometimes young killer whales get pimples, just like humans do!

How do we tell them apart?

When John Ford answers his telephone, it might be a whale on the line! John studies the vocal sounds of killer whales on the west coast of Canada. Underwater microphones pick up the sounds, and a cellular phone system carries them to John's office. Each killer whale pod has an accent or "dialect" of different sounds. John used a sound analyzer to turn recordings of the sounds into computer images. He transformed the complex images into a code of single squiggles, which helped him to categorize the different sounds. After listening to thousands of hours of killer whale clicks, whistles and squeals, John recognizes pods better than his computer can.

John Ford tells killer whales apart by voices, but twenty-five years ago researchers couldn't tell them apart at all. Then, killer whale sightings suggested there must be thousands of whales. But what if people were seeing the same whales over and over again? Now researchers identify individual killer whales by their dorsal fins. The fins are in photo-identification catalogues that look like school yearbooks—but all the photos are of fins, not faces!

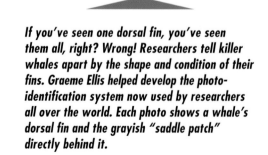

If you've seen one dorsal fin, you've seen them all, right? Wrong! Researchers tell killer whales apart by the shape and condition of their fins. Graeme Ellis helped develop the photo-identification system now used by researchers all over the world. Each photo shows a whale's dorsal fin and the grayish "saddle patch" directly behind it.

Killer whales stay with their mothers a long time, so it's easy for researchers to match up the whales with their mothers. But it's almost impossible to tell who killer whale fathers are. Killer whales breed underwater, and it isn't certain that anyone has ever seen a wild killer whale mating. The only way to identify fathers is to take samples of tissue from whales and analyze the cells to find out which males and calves share the same genes. Lance Barrett-Lennard is a researcher involved in this kind of study.

Lance wanted to test whales that were probably related, to increase the chances he'd find matching genes. He had to find the whales along a vast stretch of rocky coastline in British Columbia and Alaska. Lance and marine mammal researchers Kathy Heise (who happens to be Lance's wife) and Graeme Ellis spent long hours in rough weather for three summers searching for the whales and waiting for the chance to collect skin samples. Now Lance is at work in the laboratory, running chemical tests to find the genetic make-up of nearly one hundred samples. With the help of a computer sorting program, he'll search through the hundreds and hundreds of possible combinations to try to find which fathers and calves match.

A Family Album of Fins

All the photos used for killer whale photo-identification show the left side of the whale. Like you, a whale's left side is not exactly the same as its right. The photographs are always taken from the same side to make it easier to compare one whale with another.

Researchers (from left to right) Lance Barrett-Lennard, Graeme Ellis and Kathy Heise head out to collect a skin sample from a killer whale. Lance, holding the dart used to take the sample, has to get close enough to a whale to touch it. The dart (see inset photo) removes a piece of skin about the size of the eraser on a pencil.

How do different groups live?

Amazingly, killer whales that live in different parts of the world "speak" different languages, eat different foods, use different hunting techniques and live in different kinds of families. Along the coastline of British Columbia alone, there are three completely different types of killer whales.

The easiest type of BC killer whale to identify is the fish-eating *resident*. Each summer, nearly three hundred residents follow the salmon migration along the coast. They live in pods of up to fifty whales, sharing a common "language" of sounds. In the same area, *transient* killer whales cruise the shoreline in smaller groups, hunting for warm-blooded animals. Their language and hunting techniques are completely different from those of residents. Even though resident and transient killer whales travel the same coastline, they avoid each other's company.

For twenty years, scientists only knew of two groups of killer whales along Canada's west coast. Then, in 1989, gray whale researchers spotted some killer whales. They took underwater sound recordings and photo-identification shots, and gave their findings to killer whale researchers. The whales turned out to be a third completely different type! These *offshore* killer whales are still incredibly tough to find, but the work of researchers and whale watchers has gathered photo identification of more than two hundred offshore killer whales.

These resident killer whales can swallow buckets of fish in a single gulp. They normally do it underwater, so how do we figure out what they're eating? Researchers studying killer whale diets have become pros at handling scoop nets. As soon as they see whales hunting, they speed over in their boats to collect fish parts that float to the surface. By playing fish-scale detectives, researchers have found that each pod of resident killer whales feeds on a different type of salmon, and doesn't compete with other pods for the same food.

A Meal Fit for a Whale

Researchers dissect dead whales that wash up on shore to find out what they eat. Sometimes they find the bones, teeth and hair of deer in the stomachs of dead transient killer whales. The deer try to swim between islands, and are nabbed by whales as an easy meal.

This killer whale from Patagonia, Argentina, must hunt silently. Any sound would easily be detected by the seals, sea lions and other whales that it hopes to catch. When it does make a kill, it's over in the blink of an eye! In this group, females sometimes teach young whales to hunt. Scientists watched as a female killer whale charged the beach with a two-year-old in tow, and then tossed a sea lion pup back to the eager young student.

At the Crozet Islands off the tip of South Africa, you can see killer whales lunge onto shore like surfers riding a wave onto the beach. Quick as a flash, they scoop up baby elephant seals and slip back into the sea. These hunters run the risk of being stranded when the waves go out. So the mothers teach their calves how to beach themselves. When the youngsters are two-year-olds, their mothers shove them onto the backs of other whales and even onto the beach to give them the experience of being out of water. By the age of five, calves can catch elephant seal pups, but they can't get themselves back into the water without a shoulder push from mom. It's not until a young whale is eight or nine years old that it can time its beach attacks well enough to catch a pup and retreat without help.

Are they in danger?

One of the hardest things about studying whales is figuring out what is "usual" and what is not. This knowledge is crucial if we want to learn how human activity affects whales. If we know where they usually travel, we can tell when they change their routes. If we know a group is healthy, we can look for changes in the environment that cause them to become sick and die. If we know what they normally eat, we will be able to see what happens if their diet gets scarce. Researchers try to see if the changes we make to the world have put whales in danger.

Scientists are concerned about the effect of water pollution on fish, and on the killer whales that eat them. Using the small amount of blubber collected with the skin samples used by Lance Barrett-Lennard, Graeme Ellis and his colleagues examine the health of killer whale calves and their mothers. They have confirmed that levels of some poisons are higher in calves than in mothers. That's because the pollutants that build up in a mother's blubber are passed through her milk to her nursing calf.

These resident killer whales return every year to Johnstone Strait, British Columbia. A few summers ago, they never showed up! Were they frightened away by the noise of boats filled with whale watchers? Turns out that fish, not boats, changed the whales' routine. A shift in warm water currents caused the salmon the whales eat (see left) to move to a different area, and the whales followed their prey. A year later the fish, and the whales, were back in their regular site.

Fishing for Answers

Studying fish behavior is important when we study whales. Scientists worry that overfishing by people is reducing the amount of fish available for killer whales to eat. Do killer whales switch to other kinds of fish when salmon become too hard to find? Or will the loss of salmon cause the loss of killer whales?

Environmental problems affecting whales are difficult to study because scientists first need to answer basic questions about whales. Take noise pollution—underwater noise from boats is so loud and frequent that scientists worry it will harm whale communication, hunting and navigation. We need to know what killer whales hear, and how, to know for sure.

How do you test a killer whale's hearing? Researcher David Bain enlisted the help of three female killer whales in a California aquarium. The whales wait near an underwater speaker. When they hear a tone, they swim to another station. It took lots of practice and praise to teach the whales to move only if they hear a tone. And it took hundreds of trials before researchers were sure that the whales were responding to the test. Dave then fitted electrodes into soft suction cups placed on the whales' heads, to let him "see" changes in the pattern of a whale's brain waves when it hears a tone. Brain waves may turn out to be a way to study whale hearing in the wild!

Whale Research Tomorrow

How does a beluga ever find the next breathing hole when it's travelling beneath thick arctic ice? A British research team fitted belugas with small transmitters and tracked their movements via satellite. It appears that belugas begin by making deep dives, often to depths deeper than any skyscraper! The belugas time their dives so that they are at the deepest point when they have used up half their air. Then, they use either their eyesight or their sonar (the researchers aren't sure which) to scan the ice above for distant openings. If there is an opening, they continue. If not, they head back to the original breathing hole with exactly enough air to get them back safely. These tracking techniques can be used to learn much more about other kinds of whales, too.

Another recent technique, which identifies individual whales by taking tiny samples of their skin, means researchers can study which whales are related to each other. The more we learn about the relationships between whale mothers, fathers, sisters and brothers, the more we can understand how whale communities are organized. Researchers studying killer whales off the coast of British Columbia realized that resident killer whale families have been returning to rub on the same pebbly beaches for generation after generation. Using this information, they were able to prevent the beach from being destroyed by logging and to turn it into a protected area for whales.

Lights! Camera! Sea Lions? A team of researchers working along the coast of California has come up with a novel way to study gray whale migration. They strap a backpack containing an underwater video camera to a sea lion! By training a group of sea lions to follow the movements of migrating gray whales, the scientists have created underwater movies of gray whales shot by some of the best underwater swimmers in the world.

Would you like to study whales? Many of the people in this book began dreaming about becoming whale researchers when they were your age. Some grew up on a coast where they could walk to a beach and search for blows. Others lived in towns or cities where they developed their observation and questioning skills by studying birds and small mammals in their backyards or neighborhood parks. A few didn't even know they were interested in sea life until they went on a school trip to the ocean. Today, many of these men and women share their love of whales with their own children. As families, they spend time together in boats, in the library and on the Internet searching for new questions and answers about their favorite animals. There are lots of ways to learn more about whales and whale research—just by reading this book, you've already made a start!

But do you think researchers will know everything there is to know about whales before you can grow up and study them? Never fear. There are still lifetimes of questions to be answered about the five types of whales featured in this book, and there are dozens of different kinds of whales that have rarely been *seen*, let alone studied. Each time a researcher invents a new way to study whales, it allows other researchers to explore new questions.

Acknowledgments

Very special thanks to the researchers who shared their stories for this book:

David Bain
Dave knew he wanted to be a marine biologist when he attended a National Science Foundation summer school training program as a high school student. He started working with dolphins and whales in marine parks while attending university and continues to do his research in both aquarium and wild settings. Dave likes to spend time with big animals—when he isn't studying whales he enjoys working with elephants!

Lance Barrett-Lennard and Kathy Heise
Lance and Kathy began their whale-watching careers as lighthouse keepers. When fellow researchers John Ford and Graeme Ellis asked if they would mind if they set up a hydrophone to monitor whales in the area, Lance and Kathy agreed. Their enthusiasm for marine life led them to return to university to pursue higher degrees in science and they've been keeping track of whales and other marine mammals ever since.

Jim Darling
Jim believes that to protect marine life you need good research and good political decisions. In addition to creating a marine research station in the town where he lives, Jim has also been the town councillor.

Meghan Donahue
Meghan lives near the beach where she likes to explore tide pools and kelp beds. She started thinking about becoming a marine biologist when she was in the fourth grade, but it wasn't until she finished college that her plans turned into action. When she isn't studying migrating gray whales, Meghan enjoys learning new languages and curling up with a good book.

Greg Dye
Greg isn't the only one in his family with a passion for working with whales. His wife, Meg, two of his brothers and both their wives work for aquariums too!

Graeme Ellis
Graeme (on left) has been studying marine mammals along the coast of British Columbia since he was a boy. Whether it's battling hurricane force winds to collect sea lion droppings on an isolated rookery or spending long hours at sea waiting to photograph whales, Graeme's work, along with his knowledge, patience and good humor have helped countless research projects succeed.

John Ford
John became interested in the sounds whales make when he was a young teenager volunteering at an aquarium. He and his wife met on a whale-watching boat. Together, with their children, they have travelled to whale research locations all over the world.

Fred Sharpe

Fred loves to combine his interest in marine life with his talent as an artist. His research notebooks (see photo on page 38) are filled with illustrations of whale flukes, oyster shells, wildflowers and mountains—a gallery of coastal life.

Wayne Perryman

Like most whale researchers, Wayne spends a lot of time on boats. In fact, he became a researcher after he retired from his job as the captain of a ship! When the water is choppy you'll still find him heading for the sea—ready to surf the waves in his kayak.

Index